101 OUTRAGEOUS THINGS to do on your BIRTHDAY

Written by **Matthew S. Kavet**

Illustrated by **Martin Riskin**

Layout by **CoffeyCup Productions**

©1998 by **Boston America Corp.**

No portion of this book may be reproduced - mechanically, electronically, or by any other means including photocopying - without the permission of the publisher.

30 29 28 27 26 25 24 23 22 21 20 19 18 17 16 15 14 13 12 11 10 9 8 7 6 5 4 3 2

Boston America Corp.

125 Walnut Street, Watertown, MA 02472   (617) 923-1111   FAX: (617) 923-8839

1. ☐   Buy a 3 lb bag of M&M's. Eat them all by yourself except for the red ones.

2. ☐   Go to the head of a line. **Go through the express register even if you have more than 10 items.** Tell them it's your birthday.

3. ☐ Set up a "make your own" sundae stand for your party with all your favorite flavors and toppings. Start eating it before anyone comes. When it starts to melt and run off the table announce it's time to open your presents.

4. ☐ Have an Orgy. **Getting an orgy started is the tough part,** but from then on it's all fun except for the rug burns. If you succeed give me a call.

5. ☐ **Stay naked all day.** Go to a nudist colony. Stare back at people. If you must go outside I hope you live in a warm, liberal place.

6. ☐ Buy a case of weird foreign beers. Taste them all. Only recycle the bottles you can take back to Europe.

7. ❏ Skip your workouts. Skip your vitamins. Don't weigh yourself. **Decide you're going to wear loose baggy clothing for the rest of your life.**

8. ☐ Wear a silly hat to work. Don't take it off when the boss comes in. Tell him you probably won't be here for your next birthday. Start looking for a new job if he doesn't beg you to stay.

9. ☐ **Buy a really expensive wine.** If you like, drink it all by yourself. Pretend you can taste the difference. Buy a case and stash it away for a special birthday. Then if you feel like it, drink that also.

10. ☐ Eat a meal of all your favorite things from when you were a kid. Suck on a lollipop. Chew bubble gum.

11. ☐ Set your alarm for the regular time and then shut it off and go back to sleep. When you finally wake up **stay under the covers for an hour, scratching your private parts.**

12. ☐ Tell your kids they have to feed themselves for the day. Also dress themselves, get to school and soccer practice, and do their own homework. Lock yourself in a bathroom.

13. ☐ **Don't do any dishes.** Let them pile up along with the dirty laundry and ironing. Don't make beds. You can do it all tomorrow or maybe the day after.

14. ☐ **Go to work without wearing any underwear.** Tell everyone.

15. ☐ Buy a dozen magazines on all sorts of subjects you've always been interested in. Buy some dirty ones. Send for all the free offers. See how much junk mail you get for the rest of your life.

16. ❏ **Do something kinky.** Something that's so far out you've never even considered it before. Be daring. Find someone to do it with. Don't give them your real name.

17. ☐ Bake a batch of chocolate chip cookies. Eat them all by yourself while they're still hot.

18. ☐ Drink directly from the bottles in your refrigerator. **Drink directly from the faucet.** Don't turn off lights. Let the screen door bang.

19. ☐ Go off your diet just for the day (and then don't go back on it). Buy more baggy clothes.

20. ☐ **Throw your underwear on the floor.** Leave it there. When you start to trip on the stuff, shove it under the bed.

21. ☐ Don't stop for red lights...

but don't get killed going through the intersections. I don't need any more lawsuits. If the police stop you just tell them it's your birthday and that I said it was okay but don't give them my address.

22. ☐ Have sex in the morning. Roll over and go back to sleep. **Wake up and be in a grouchy mood all day.**

23. ☐ Bet more than you can afford on a real long shot. If you win let your bet ride.

24. ☐ Go to a kind of ethnic restaurant that you've never eaten at before. Tell them it's your birthday and let the waiter order for you.

25. ☐ Have a stripper come to your party. Join in and take your clothes off. Apologize to everyone the next day, when you are sober.

26. ❑ Do you live or work in a high building? **Drop stuff out the window.** Pretend you're working, if the police come.

27. ❑ Wear your mate's underwear.
Make love with the lights on and try not to close your eyes.

28. ❑ Buy the big bag of potato chips at lunch. Don't share.

29. ☐ Have a massage from a very attractive member of the opposite sex. Don't be embarrassed if you get turned on.

30. ☐ **Don't flush.** Don't put the seat up or down. Don't replace an empty toilet paper roll. Don't apologize if you stink up the bathroom.

31. ☐ Fart in a crowded place.
Admit you did it. Say it's a birthday custom in your family.

32. ☐ Drive straddling 2 lanes. Tailgate.
Stay in the left-hand lane. Drive with your blinkers still on. Honk at anybody whose driving annoys you. (You know, just like you always do.)

33. ☐ If you're a guy, climax without waiting for your partner. Roll over and go to sleep.

34. ❑ If you're a woman insist on 2 hours of foreplay. Make him talk about love for an hour afterwards.

35. ❑ If it's sunny go to the beach. Suck in your stomach. **Wear dark glasses and ogle the bodies** of people much younger than you.

36. ☐ Have a mate or lover rub you all over with massage oil. Cooking oil probably works just as well but **it's a real mess to get it off the sheets and mattress.** This is a game that's best played at a hotel.

37. ☐ Withdraw the maximum amount of daily cash your ATM allows. Buy yourself presents.

38. ☐ Stay in the shower until all the hot water is used up. Use lots of towels. Let the water drip on the floor.

39. ☐ Take up two parking spaces. **Park in a loading zone.** Park in a reserved spot. Double park. Don't put money in a meter.

40. ☐ **Have sex with someone entirely new.** Someone you hardly know. How? Try reading my book "How To Have Sex On Your Birthday". Who knows, it might even work for you.

41. ☐
Buy a quart of your favorite ice cream flavor. Coffee Heathbar Crunch is good. Eat it right out of the container making tunnels and shapes as you pick out the good pieces.

42. ☐
Rub up against someone in an elevator or bus. If they're shocked, look indignant, and tell them it's your birthday. If they smile go home with them.

43. ☐ **Pick your nose while you drive to work.** Yes, I know you do that every day, but for your birthday flick the boogers at other drivers.

44. ☐ Spend a whole week's salary on lottery tickets. Play numbers that involve your birthday. If you win send me 10%. Hey, it was my idea.

45. ☐ Carefully read your horoscope. Follow its suggestions. Go to a fortune teller. Believe whatever she tells you.

46. ☐ Absolutely refuse to have sex if you don't feel like it. Refuse to fake an orgasm. Refuse to say how good it was for you.

47. ☐ If you've never done it before, **moon someone.**

48. ☐ Try a totally new and complicated sex position that you found in a book. Make an appointment with your chiropractor.

49. ☐ Soak in a hot tub. Listen to your favorite music. Eat an ice cream concoction. Do them all at the same time. Leave a ring in the tub.

50. ☐ **Play with the TV remote.** Switch channels spontaneously. Watch the tawdry pay-per-view stuff.

51. ☐ Go out to a really elegant dinner with your friends. Order all the things that are really too expensive. When they go to pay say, "Oh, you shouldn't have".

52. ☐ Get an erection in a place where you shouldn't and don't be embarrassed or try to hide it. Don't attempt this unless you are a man.

53. ☐ **Have multiple orgasms.** Have them all day. Let your body vibrate in peals of joy. Allow the thundering, bursting, tingling, throbbing, sensations wave over you. Don't try this unless you are a woman.

54. ☐ Forget about condoms for the day. Heh, heh heh, just kidding. I get enough threatening letters as it is, with these books.

55. ☐ **Rearrange your office so no one can see when you're playing video games** or fooling around on the internet. Goof off all day.

56. ☐ Phone friends you haven't spoken to in years. Talk for hours. Remind them it's your birthday. Maybe next year they'll send a present.

57. ☐   Send yourself flowers at work. All your co-workers will be so jealous. Yeah, it's better if a lover sends them but you can seldom count on lovers.

58. ☐   **In the evening, play some kind of sex fantasies** like "Whipped Cream Swimming Pool" or "Rubber Band Bondage" or "Lashed With Wet Linguine" or "Oh, Mr. Iceman". Find willing playmates. If they laugh at you tell them you won't invite them to next year's birthday party.

59. ☐ **Lose your virginity.** This may not sound outrageous to you perverts out there who have already lost yours but to some people it's a very special thing. If you have already lost your virginity you can try to find it. Look in the back seat of cars, under blankets at the beach, and in the couches of living rooms.

60. ☐ Wear some totally unreasonable article of intimate apparel under your regular clothes.

61. ☐ **Have your car washed.** Hell, it's your birthday, have it waxed and detailed. Fill it with premium gas and get new wiper blades. Write HAPPY BIRTHDAY across the back window with shaving cream and then ride around and honk at people you'd like to pick up.

62. ☐ Listen to your kind of music. Don't turn it down when people complain. Sing along. Whistle.

63. ☐ E-mail everyone on your list with a general letter thanking all of them for the warm thoughts, birthday wishes and gifts. Next year you should clean up.

64. ☐ **Make a deal with God** that if he will just let you once win the lottery real big or make your number or horse come in, you will go to your place of worship at least every other week.

65. ☐ Have sex in a new imaginative place like a waterbed smothered in strawberries or a bathtub filled with oatmeal or on plastic sheets drenched in chocolate. Let your imagination soar. Shower afterwards.

66. ☐ Call a childhood sweetheart. See if you can get things going again.

67. ☐ At each meal today make sure you get at least 2 of the desserts from the 5 major dessert groups:

Ice Cream *Chocolate Cake*
Cream Pies *Strawberry cheesecake*
Candy made with peanut butter

Put frosting on your nose and try to lick it off.

68. ☐ Take a nap at work. Go out for a really long lunch. Leave for home early.

69. ☐ **Tie birthday ribbons all over your dog.**

70. ☐ Invite your cat to your birthday party.

71. ☐ Don't pay any bills. Anyone calling for money today should be told in a firm voice that it's your birthday and you don't handle financial transactions.

72. ☐ Do things you haven't done since you were a kid. Fly a kite, climb a tree, make a slingshot, play with yourself in the bathroom.

73. ☐ If you've recently stopped smoking, this is a good day to just **enjoy a few puffs for old times' sake.**

74. ☐ **Go into a sex shop and buy something** you've always wanted to buy but never would dare. Wear a disguise if you must. Carry it home in a plain paper bag.

75. ☐ Get tanked at a Happy Hour. Eat all the free chicken wings. Cut the toilet line. Let your friends pick up all the tab.

76. ☐ Plant a little tree. Then every year on your birthday you can go out and see how much it's grown.

77. ☐ Call your parents. Thank them for all the things they've done for you all through your life. (I'm just writing this on the off chance my own kids will read it.)

78. ☐ Make a list of all the important things that you just have to get done today. Then don't do any of them.

79. ☐ Jump up and down in an elevator. Make faces and wave your arms. Compose yourself just before the doors open.

80. ☐ E-mail the President, Governor and other high officials expressing concern over not getting a birthday card this year. I'll bet they send one next year especially if they're up for reelection.

81. ☐ **Tell someone you love them.** Make a commitment. If later, you want to change your mind, it's okay because it was your birthday.

82. ☐ Throw out your arms as you meet people at work. Say it's your birthday. See how many hugs you get.

83. ☐ **Do something one time for each year of your life.** Be imaginative; drinks work nicely up to a certain age; kisses are much better.

84. ☐ Start your birthday early; stay up all night.
Watch the sunrise. Drink specialty coffee. Keep going until midnight and finish with brandy and cigars.

85. ☐ Try on clothes for hours. Buy a really wild outfit. Return it the next day.

86. ☐ Throw out all your torn underwear. Go to work without socks.

87. ☐ Buy 10 candy bars and hide them around your home and office. Eat them whenever you find one.

88. ☐ Tell people it's your birthday and then pucker up. Almost everyone will kiss you. Try it with strangers.

89. ☐ Order way too much food at a Chinese restaurant. Give the leftovers to a homeless person. **Teach them to use chopsticks.**

90. ☐ Open all your presents. Rip off the wrappings in a hurry. Don't let anyone else play with them.

91. ☐ **Rearrange your furniture.** Redecorate a room with an outrageous poster. Throw out an old rug.

92. ☐ Pretend you are a voyeur.
Maybe you are. Spend the day with a telescope peeking in people's windows.

93. ☐ Climb up to a high spot. Spit.

94. ☐ Hang up on all the telephone solicitors. Even better, don't answer your phone. Don't return calls. Leave a message on your machine telling everyone about your birthday.

95. ☐ Take the time to read the entire newspaper.

96. ☐ Sleep the way you want. Sleep with the windows open. Sleep with them closed. **Sleep naked** or outside or in front of the TV. Don't share the blankets.

97. ☐ Don't take any crap from surly waiters, service personnel, sales clerks and mechanics.

98. ☐ Don't floss. **Don't brush after every meal.**

99. ☐ Buy an extra jelly donut with your coffee.

100. ☐ Forget to shave. Don't pluck your eyebrows, ear or nose hairs. Wear comfy old shoes.

101. ☐ Lie about your age. Lie when people ask, "which birthday". Do it every year and you'll see how you never grow old.

OTHER GREAT BOOKS BY BOSTON AMERICA

The fine cultivated stores carrying our books really get ticked if you buy direct from the publisher so, if you can, please patronize your local store and let them make a buck. If, however, the fools don't carry a particular title, you can order them from us for $8 postpaid. Credit cards accepted for orders of 3 or more books.

#2700 Rules For Sex On Your Wedding Night
All the rules from undressing the bride to ensuring the groom will respect her in the morning.

#2703 You Know You're A Golf Addict When...
You hustle your grandmother, watch golf videos and think you look good in golf clothes.

#2704 What Every Woman Can Learn From Her Cat
You'll learn that an unmade bed is fluffier and there's no problem that can't be helped by a nap among many others.

#2705 Adult Connect The Dots
If you can count to 100 and hold a pencil you can draw really sexy pictures of people doing "you know what".

#2706 Is There Sex After 50?
Everything from swapping for two-25-year olds to finding out it's not sexy tucking your T-shirt into your underpants.

#2707 Beer Is Better Than Women Because...
Beers don't change their minds once you take off their tops and don't expect an hour of foreplay.

#2708 You Know You're Over 30 When...
You start wearing underwear almost all of the time and no longer have to lie on your resume.

#2709 You Know You're Over 40 When...
You feel like the morning after and you can swear you haven't been anywhere and you start to look forward to dull evenings at home.

#2710 You Know You're Over 50 When...
Your arms aren't long enough to hold your reading material and you sit down to put on your underwear.

#2711 You Know You're Over The Hill When...
No one cares any more what you did in high school and you see your old cereal bowl in an antique shop.

#2712 Birthdays Happen
Your biological urges have dwindled to an occasional nudge and you discuss "regularity" at your birthday party.

#2713 Unspeakable Farts
These are the ones that were only whispered about in locker rooms like the "Hold Your Breath Fart" and "The Morning Fart".

#2714 101 Great Drinking Games
A remarkable collection of fun and creative drinking games including all the old favorites and many new ones you can barely imagine.

#2715 How To Have Sex On Your Birthday
Finding a partner, the birthday orgasm, birthday sex games and much more.

#2717 Women Over 40 Are Better Because...
They are smart enough to hire someone to do the cleaning and men at the office actually solicit their advice.

#2718 Women Over 50 Are Better Because...
They don't fall to pieces if you see them without their makeup and are no longer very concerned about being "with it".

#2719 Is There Sex After 40?
Great cartoons analyzing this important subject from sexy cardigans to the bulge that used to be in his trousers.

#2720 Plop
Let's just say this book is a favorite of teenage boys who find the toilet humor about the funniest thing they can imagine.

#2721 Cucumbers Are Better Than Men Because...
They won't make a pass at your friends, don't care if you shave your legs and stay hard for a week.

#2722 Better An Old Fart Than A Young Shithead
A great comparison of the Old Fart who dresses for comfort and the Young Shithead who is afraid of looking like a dork.

#2723 101 Outrageous Things To Do On Your Birthday
Wear a silly hat to work, jump up and down in an elevator, don't wear any underwear and drive straddling 2 lanes.

#2724 My Favorite Teacher
A super gift for a teacher that shows how to handle April Fools Day and outsmart kids who are smarter than the teacher.

#2725 My Favorite Nurse
A gift for nurses that explains how they make doctors look good, eject obnoxious visitors, and keep from getting sick.

#2726 Your New Baby
This is a manual that explains everything from unpacking your new baby to handling kids' plumbing and routine servicing.

#2727 Diddle Your Way To Success With Women
This book teaches how diddling works, basic techniques, first time diddling and how to know when to stop.

#2728 Sex After Retirement
Everyone needs a gift for retiring friends and this riotous cartoon book is perfect to help the retiree while away the hours.

#2729 Great Bachelor Parties
This book tells it all from finding a cooperative stripper to getting rid of the father-in-law to damage control with the bride to be.

#2730 Rules For Engaged Couples
Rules for living together, meeting the family, learning to share and planning the wedding.

#2731 The Bachelorette Party
Great pre-party and party ideas and suggestions for everything from limos to outfits to strippers to your behavior in bars.

#2732 Brides Guide To Sex And Marriage
Dealing with your husband's family and learning what he does in the bathroom and secrets of sleeping comfortably together.

#2403 The Good Bonking Guide
Bonking is a very useful British term for "you know what" and this book covers bonking in the dark, bonking all night long and more.

#2434 Sex And Marriage
Make your wife more exciting in bed and teach your husband about romance. Hobbies, religion and getting a husband to fix your car.

#2501 Cowards Guide To Body Piercing
Cartoons and explanations of all the good and horrible places you can put holes in yourself.

#1500 Fish Tank Video $15 postpaid
This fish tank video enables you to experience all the joys of beautiful, colorful and graceful tropical fish without having to care for them. You'll find yourself hypnotized by the delicate beauty of these fish. Approximately 1 hour running time.

BOSTON AMERICA C★O★R★P

125 Walnut Street, Watertown, MA 02472   (617) 923-1111   FAX: (617) 923-8839